This Book Belongs
to

SANTA EXPRESS
TRAIN TIMES

LETTERS

(Answer on page 46)

TOY SHOP
SUGAR & SPICE
Cafe
GIFTS FOR ALL AGES
TOY SHOP
OPEN LATE
HOLIDAY TOY DRIVE TODAY!

RRY CHRISTM

OULIN ROUGE

PIZZERIA
PIZZA
PASTA
LASAGNA
SPAGHETTI
LUNCH SPECIALS $7

Ava's Bridal Shop
Ava's
MR
&
MR

(Answer on page 46)

SANTA EXPRESS
TRAIN TIMES